ANIMAL JOKES FOR FUNNY KIDS

Buster Books

Illustrated by
Andrew Pinder

Compiled by Josephine Southon

Edited by Emma Taylor

Designed by Derrian Bradder

First published in Great Britain in 2021 by Buster Books,
an imprint of Michael O'Mara Books Limited,
9 Lion Yard, Tremadoc Road, London SW4 7NQ

W www.mombooks.com/buster   f Buster Books   🐦 @BusterBooks   📷 @buster_books

A CIP catalogue record for this book is available from the British Library.

ISBN: 978-1-78055-784-7
2 4 6 8 10 9 7 5 3

Papers used by Buster Books are natural, recyclable products made of wood from
well-managed, FSC®-certified forests and other controlled sources. The manufacturing
processes conform to the environmental regulations of the country of origin.

Printed and bound in March 2022 by CPI Group (UK) Ltd,
108 Beddington Lane, Croydon, CR0 4YY, United Kingdom.

FSC
www.fsc.org
MIX
Paper from
responsible sources
FSC® C171272

CONTENTS

Introduction

Why do owls always get
invited to parties?

Because they're a hoot!

Welcome to this te he he-larious collection
of the best-ever animal jokes for funny kids.

In this book you will find over 300 pawsome
jokes which will have you roaring with
laughter – from rainforest rib-ticklers and
swampy side-splitters to silly sea life and
woodland wisecracks.

If these jokes don't tickle your funny bone
then nothing will. Don't forget to share your
favourites with your friends and family
and practise your comic timing!

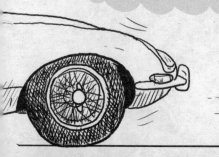

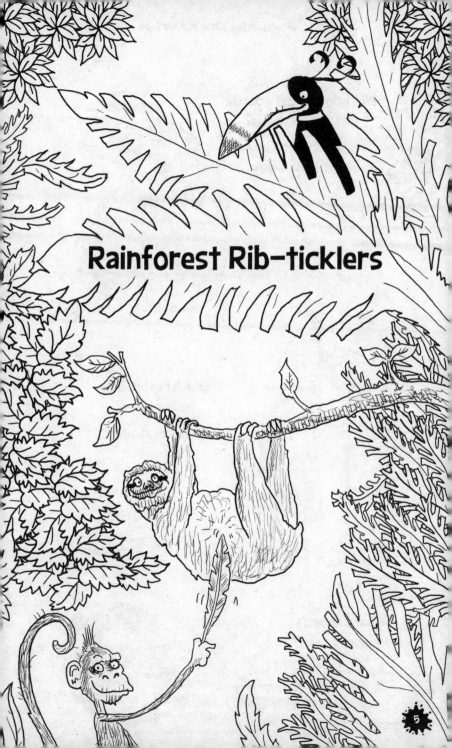

Rainforest Rib-ticklers

What do you call a gorilla wearing earmuffs?

Anything you like, it can't hear you!

Which reptile likes telling jokes?

A stand-up chameleon.

What's an ape's favourite food?

Chocolate chimp cookies.

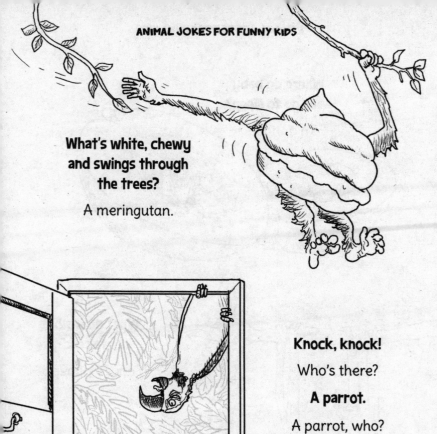

What's white, chewy and swings through the trees?

A meringutan.

Knock, knock!

Who's there?

A parrot.

A parrot, who?

A parrot, who?

What's the scariest flower in the jungle?

A tiger lily.

Where do baby apes go to sleep?

In apricots.

What do sloths like to read?

Snooze-papers.

What's orange and sounds like a parrot?

A carrot.

Why are gorillas bad at telling stories?

They have no tails.

How does a monkey get down the stairs?

It slides down the banana-ster.

What is as big as an orangutan but weighs nothing?

Its shadow.

9

What happened to the leopard that took a bath three times a day?

It was spotless.

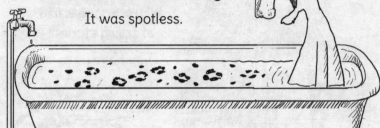

What's a chameleon's favourite kitchen tool?

A blender.

Which US president do gorillas like the most?

Ape-raham Lincoln.

Two monkeys run a bath.

One says, "Ooh ooh, ahh ahh!" The other says, "Put some cold water in it then!"

What do you get when you cross a parrot with a centipede?

A walkie talkie.

Why can't you trust a tiger?

It could be lion.

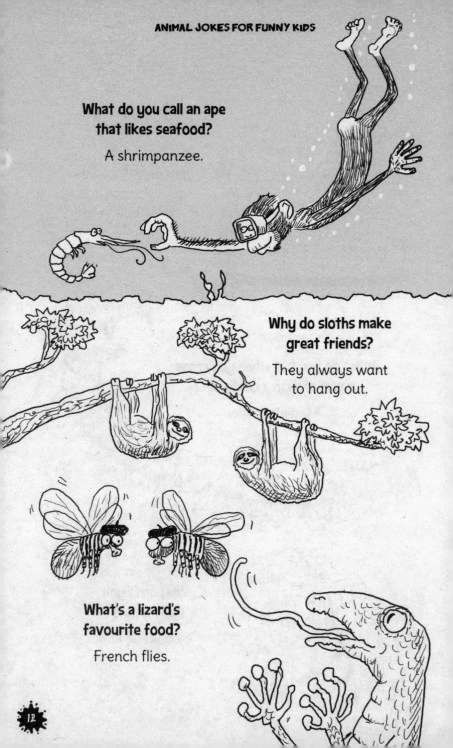

**What do you call an ape
that likes seafood?**

A shrimpanzee.

**Why do sloths make
great friends?**

They always want
to hang out.

**What's a lizard's
favourite food?**

French flies.

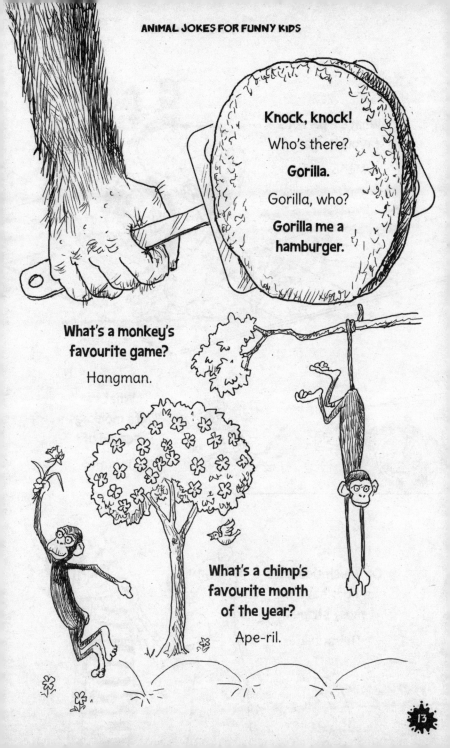

Knock, knock!

Who's there?

Gorilla.

Gorilla, who?

Gorilla me a hamburger.

What's a monkey's favourite game?

Hangman.

What's a chimp's favourite month of the year?

Ape-ril.

What's a parrot's favourite game?

Mono-polly.

What car are monkeys scared of?

Jaguars.

On which side does a tiger have the most stripes?

The outside.

Have you heard the joke about a sloth crossing the road?

Never mind, it'd take too long.

How do you make a telephone in the jungle?

With toucans and a piece of string.

What's an ape's favourite snack?

Chimps and dip.

15

What's the first thing a gorilla learns at school?

The Ape B Cs.

What do you get if you cross a parrot with a woodpecker?

A bird that talks in Morse code.

What do you call a monkey flying in the sky?

A hot-air baboon.

Why do gorillas have big nostrils?

Because they have big fingers.

Why don't tigers like fast food?

Because they can't catch it.

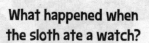

What happened when the sloth ate a watch?

It was very time consuming.

Farm
Fun

**Doctor, Doctor!
I feel like a pony.**

Don't worry, you're
only a little hoarse.

**Why aren't
chicks funny?**

They tell cheep jokes.

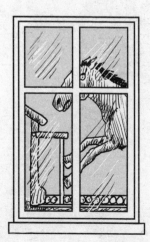

**Why did the horse practise
its galloping in private?**

It didn't want to make
a foal of itself.

How can you tell which cow is the best dancer?

It's the one with the best mooves.

What did the horse say when it fell over?

"I've fallen and I can't giddy-up!"

What do you get when you cross a chicken with an alien?

An eggs-traterrestrial.

What do you call a pig
who steals things?

A hamburglar.

What did the secret
agent cow say before
its mission?

"I'm going udder cover."

Knock, knock!

Who's there?

Goat.

Goat, who?

Goat to the door
and find out.

How do horses stay in such great shape?

They have a stable diet.

What do you call a baby goat that's good at martial arts?

The Karate Kid.

What do you call a pig who's good at karate?

Pork Chop.

What do farmers say to their cows after 9 pm?

"It's pasture bedtime."

Why wouldn't the sheepdog listen to the shepherd's jokes?

It'd herd them all before.

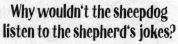

What do you get when you cross a sheep with a kangaroo?

A woolly jumper.

Where do sheep get their hair cut?

At the baa-baas.

Where did the sheep go on holiday?

The Baahamas.

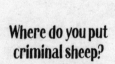

Where do you put criminal sheep?

Behind baas.

What kind of animal goes "OOM"?

A cow walking backwards.

What do you call a sleeping bull?

A bulldozer.

Why is it hard to have a conversation with a goat?

They always butt in.

Why did the horse keep sneezing?

It had hay fever.

What would happen if pigs could fly?

The price of bacon would go up.

What do you get if you're sat on by a cow?

A pat on the head.

What do chicks like to do at Halloween?

Trick or tweeting.

Why did the sheep run off the cliff?

It didn't see the ewe turn.

What do you get if you cross a pig with a dinosaur?

Jurassic Pork.

27

Why are pigs good storytellers?

There's always a twist in the tale.

Why should you never share a bed with a pig?

They always hog the covers.

Why did the pig lose the running race?

It pulled a hamstring.

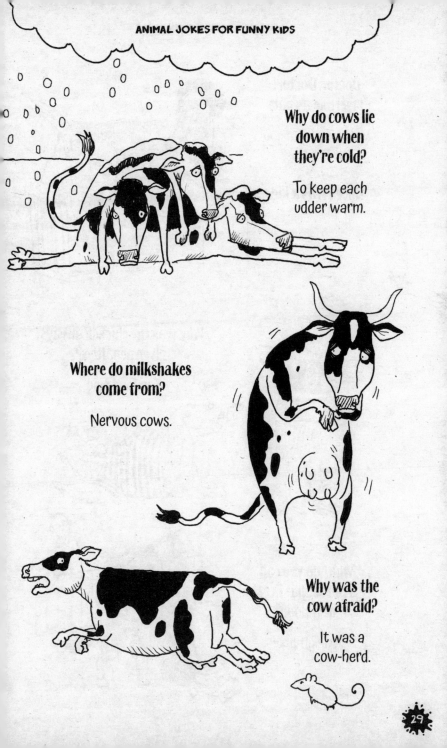

Why do cows lie down when they're cold?

To keep each udder warm.

Where do milkshakes come from?

Nervous cows.

Why was the cow afraid?

It was a cow-herd.

29

Doctor, Doctor!
I feel like a goat.

How long have you
felt like this?

Since I was a kid.

Why was the chicken always
given penalties?

For fowl play.

What do you call
a horse that lives
next door?

A neigh-bour.

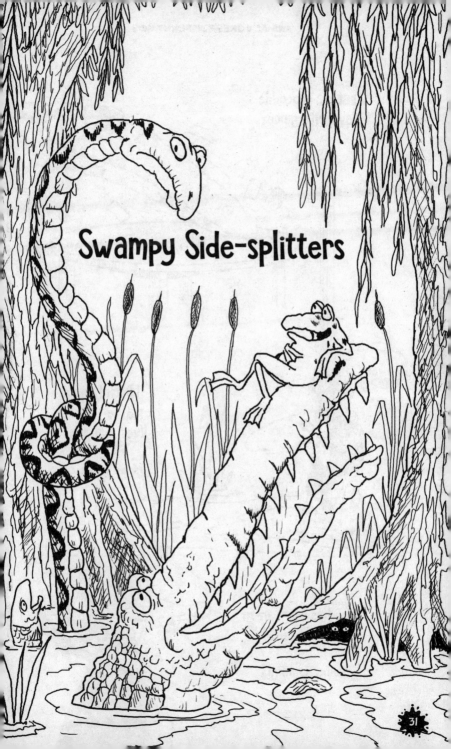

Swampy Side-splitters

What's a crocodile's favourite game?

Snap.

Which famous mathematician lives in a pond?

Isaac Newt-on.

Who has fangs and webbed feet?

Count Duckula.

What's a frog's favourite sport?

Croquet.

Why should you never play cards with an alligator?

Because you'll lose every hand.

What does a frog say when you offer it a book?

"Reddit, reddit, reddit."

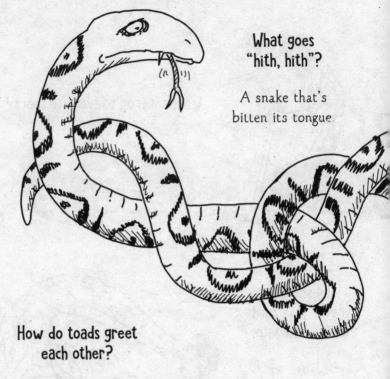

What goes "hith, hith"?

A snake that's bitten its tongue.

How do toads greet each other?

"Wart's new?"

What do you get when you cross a crocodile with a rooster?

A croc-a-doodle-doo.

What's a snake's
favourite subject?

Hisss-tory.

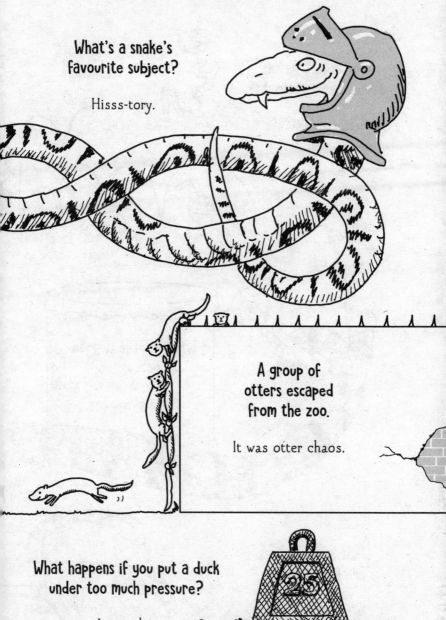

A group of
otters escaped
from the zoo.

It was otter chaos.

What happens if you put a duck
under too much pressure?

It quacks.

35

Why aren't snakes allowed energy drinks?

Because it makes them viper-active.

Which reptile is good at percussion?

A rattlesnake.

What kinds of snakes are found on cars?

Windshield vipers.

I never understand why people are afraid of snakes.

They're completely armless.

What do you call a snake that can do magic tricks?

An adder-cadabra.

Why can't you fool a snake?

You can't pull its leg.

What music do crocodiles listen to?

Croc and roll.

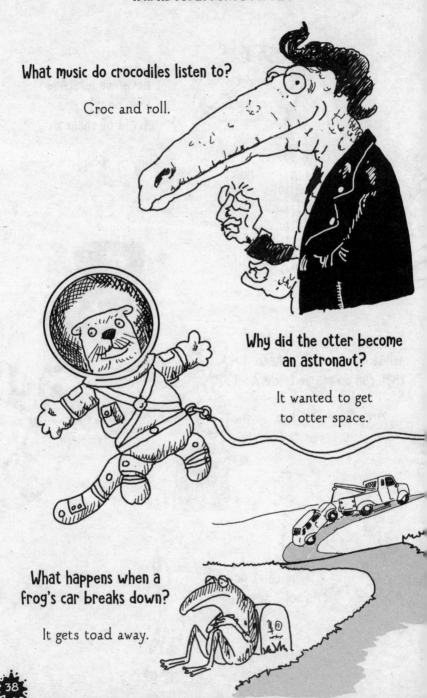

Why did the otter become an astronaut?

It wanted to get to otter space.

What happens when a frog's car breaks down?

It gets toad away.

What time does a
duck wake up?

At the quack
of dawn.

How do you address a
French female beaver?

"Ma'dam."

Why should you never
double-cross a crocodile?

It might come back
to bite you.

Why did the salamander feel lonely?

It was newt to the area.

Why are ducks so smart?

They watch lots of duck-umentaries.

What do you call an alligator wearing a vest?

An investigator.

Desert Delights

**What's sweet and
lives in the desert?**

A caramel.

**Where do scorpions
go on holiday?**

Stingapore

**What did the coyote say
to its best friend?**

"I will never desert you."

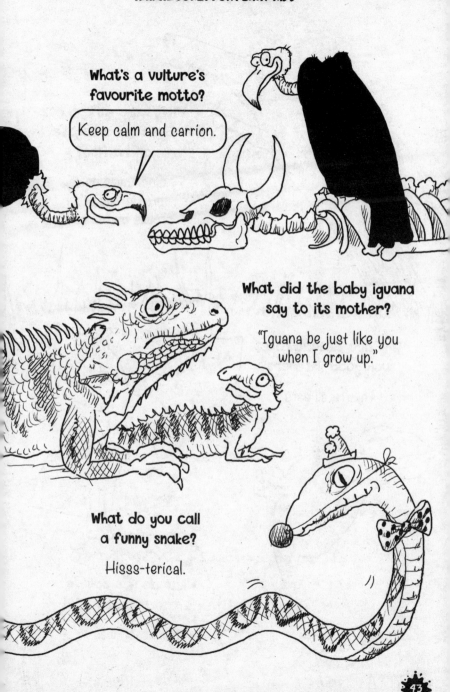

What's a vulture's favourite motto?

Keep calm and carrion.

What did the baby iguana say to its mother?

"Iguana be just like you when I grow up."

What do you call a funny snake?

Hisss-terical.

What's the difference between a coyote and a flea?

One howls on the prairie, the other prowls on the hairy.

Why are desert foxes such good listeners?

They're all ears.

What do you call a sad camel?

A humpback-wail.

**What do armadillos
say at the weekend?**

"Arma-chill-o."

**Why can't vultures
fly on planes?**

No carrion luggage allowed.

**What do you call a
camel with no humps?**

Humphrey.

What did the lizard say to the cactus?

"You're looking sharp today."

What do you call a group of superhero vultures?

The Scavengers.

What do you call an armadillo going into battle?

An armour-dillo.

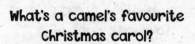

What's a camel's favourite Christmas carol?

O Camel, Ye Faithful.

Why do coyotes howl at night?

Because they can't see the cacti when it's dark.

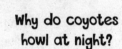

What did the scorpion say when it thought it was dreaming?

"Pinch me!"

47

What's a camel's favourite part of a meal?

Dessert.

Desert animals must be terrible at telling jokes.

Why else is there so much tumbleweed?

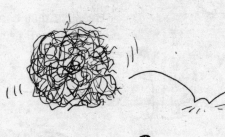

What did the coyote say when someone stepped on its paw?

"Aoooowwww!"

What's a camel's favourite nursery rhyme?

Humpty Dumpty.

Why do geckos like hip-hop music?

Because they're rap-tiles.

What did the vulture say as it flew over the Sahara Desert?

"Long time, no sea."

What's a scorpion's favourite book?

The Lord of the Stings.

Why don't animals in the desert ever go hungry?

Because of all the sand which is there.

What type of snake does a baby like to play with?

A rattlesnake.

What does a camel use to hide?

Camel-flage.

I rode a camel once.

It had its ups and downs.

What do you get if you cross a camel with a cow?

Lumpy milkshakes.

What did the pig say when it was in the desert for too long?

"I'm bacon out here!"

Why don't desert animals get dehydrated?

They're all trained in thirst-aid.

What did the llama say to the sad camel?

"Don't worry, you'll get over this hump."

What do you call a mongoose that has run away from the desert?

A gongoose.

I didn't need to go to the desert to look for an exotic spider.

It turns out there are loads of them on the web.

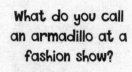

What do you call an armadillo at a fashion show?

A roll model.

Pawsome Pets

What's a dog's favourite breakfast?

Pooched eggs.

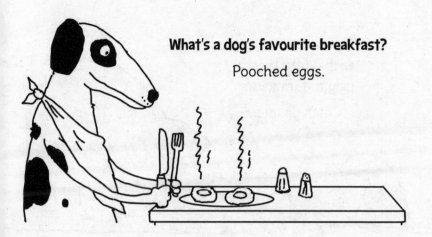

What do you call a cat that lives underwater?

An octo-puss.

What did the Dalmatian say after a nice dinner?

"That hit the spot!"

What did the lazy cat say to the mouse?

"Catch ya later."

What do you call a dog who digs up ancient artefacts?

Indiana Bones.

What did the alien say to the cat?

"Take me to your litter."

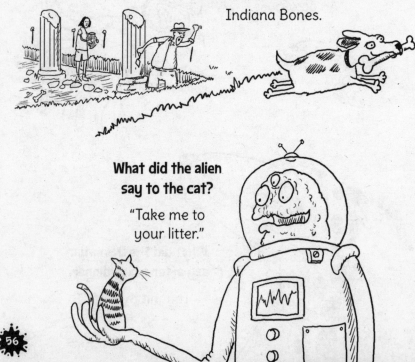

Why are cats so good at video games?

Because they have nine lives.

Where should you never take a dog?

To the flea market.

What's a rabbit's favourite style of music?

Hip-hop.

What did the guinea pig say to the stick of celery?

It's been nice gnawing you.

Where do hamsters come from?

Hamsterdam.

What's Dracula's favourite pet?

A bloodhound.

"My dog has no nose."

"How does it smell?"

"Terrible!"

Why should you be careful when it's raining cats and dogs?

You might step in a poodle.

What do you call a dog falling from a great height?

A Chihuahu-aaargh!

What kind of sports cars do cats drive?

Fur-rarris.

Where do kittens go on school trips?

The meow-seum.

What are the cat police also known as?

Claw enforcement.

What's a reptile's favourite movie?

The Lizard of Oz.

My hamster ran on its wheel for three days straight.

It was on a roll.

What do snakes do when they get angry?

They throw hissy fits.

61

What did the chameleon say to its kid on their first day of school?

"Don't worry, you'll blend right in!"

How do you know carrots are good for your eyes?

Because you never see rabbits wearing glasses!

What do dogs say before eating their dinner?

Bone Appétit!

What's a dog's favourite pizza topping?

Pup-eroni.

How do dogs train their fleas?

From scratch.

What should you do if your dog chews your dictionary?

Take the words right out of its mouth.

Why do cats always get their own way?

Because they're very purr-suasive.

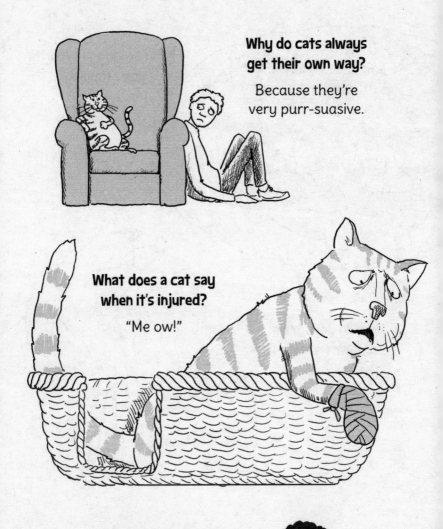

What does a cat say when it's injured?

"Me ow!"

Why did the cat see the vet?

It wasn't feline well.

What do you call a cat who commits crimes?

A purr-petrator.

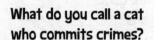

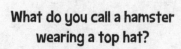

What's a butcher's favourite pet?

A sausage dog.

What do you call a hamster wearing a top hat?

Abrahamster Lincoln.

**Which snakes are good
at doing sums?**

Adders.

**What do you give to
a dog with a fever?**

Mustard – it's the best
thing for a hot dog.

**Did you hear about the cat who
swallowed a ball of wool?**

She had mittens.

Silly Sea Life

Why are fish so smart?

Because they live in schools.

Which fish only swim at night?

Starfish.

Why do fish live in saltwater?

Because pepper makes them sneeze.

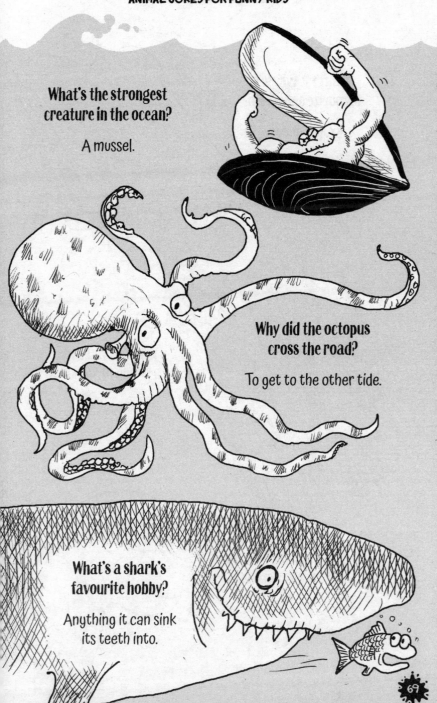

What's the strongest creature in the ocean?

A mussel.

Why did the octopus cross the road?

To get to the other tide.

What's a shark's favourite hobby?

Anything it can sink its teeth into.

69

What's a whale's favourite sandwich?

Krilled cheese.

What do you call a group of squid?

A squad.

How do dolphins make decisions?

They flipper coin.

Have you ever seen a fish cry?

No, but I've seen a whale blubber.

Where do sharks like to go on holiday?

Finland.

Why would an octopus be good in battle?

It's well-armed.

How did the mollusc get to the hospital?

In a clambulance.

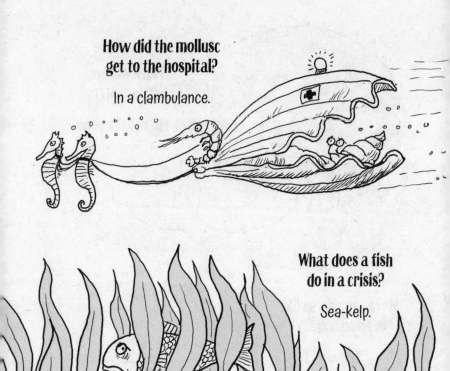

What does a fish do in a crisis?

Sea-kelp.

Why didn't the shrimp share its food?

It was a little shellfish.

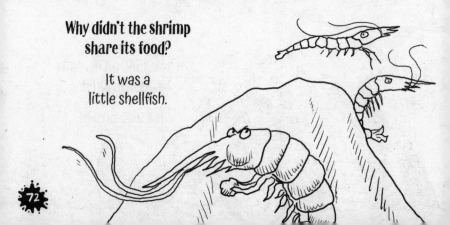

What do turtles do on their birthdays?

They shell-ebrate.

How do you make an octopus laugh?

Give it ten-tickles.

What do you call a group of musical whales?

An orca-stra.

73

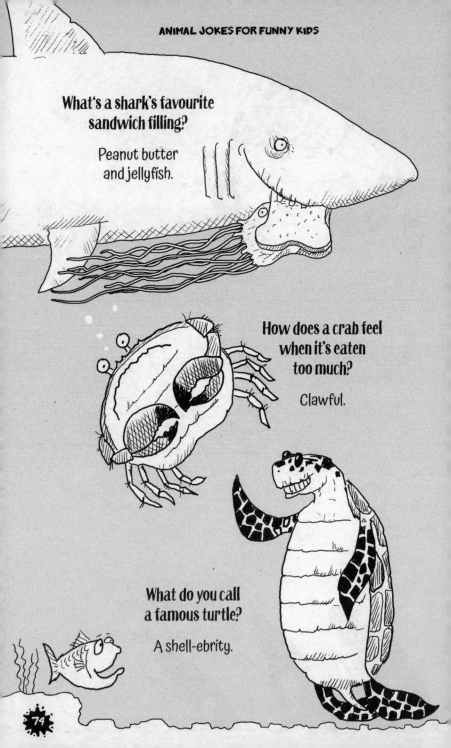

What's a shark's favourite sandwich filling?

Peanut butter and jellyfish.

How does a crab feel when it's eaten too much?

Clawful.

What do you call a famous turtle?

A shell-ebrity.

What do you call a fish without an eye?

A fsh.

How do fish get to school?

By octobus.

Why did the fish blush?

It saw the ocean's bottom.

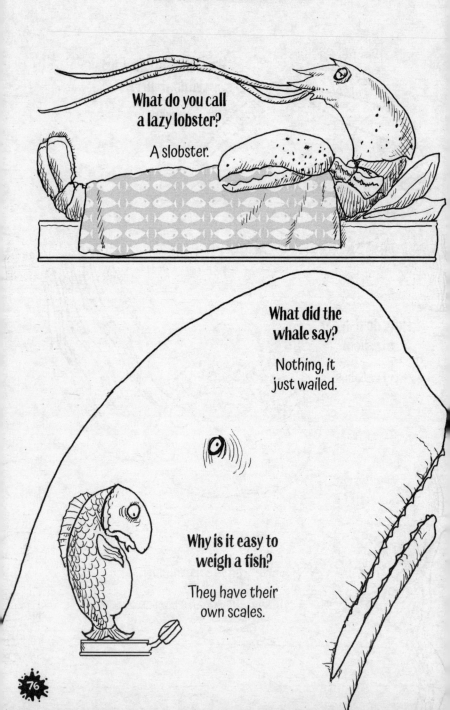

What do you call a lazy lobster?

A slobster.

What did the whale say?

Nothing, it just wailed.

Why is it easy to weigh a fish?

They have their own scales.

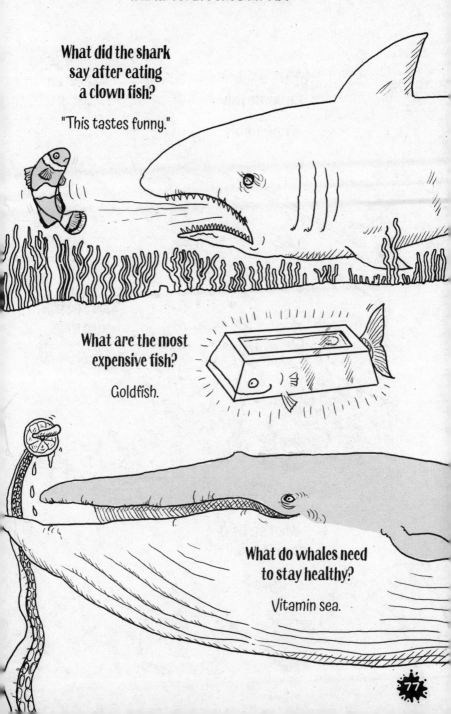

What did the shark say after eating a clown fish?

"This tastes funny."

What are the most expensive fish?

Goldfish.

What do whales need to stay healthy?

Vitamin sea.

What's a knight's favourite fish?

A swordfish.

Where do fish go to sing?

The choral reef.

What's a fish's favourite subject?

Algae-bra.

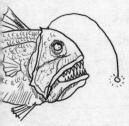

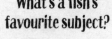

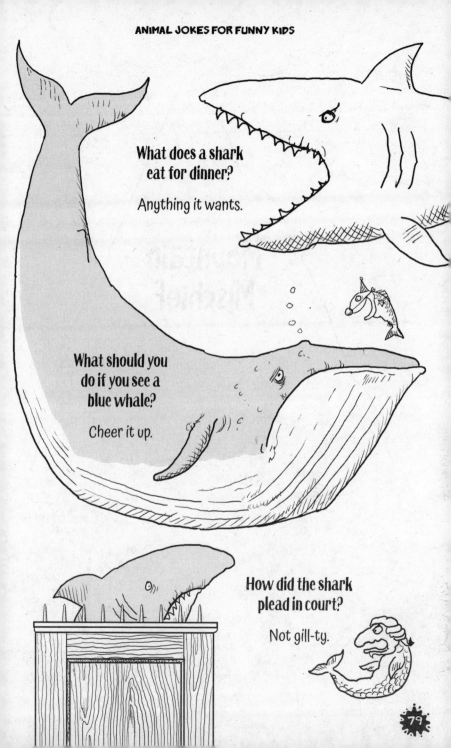

What does a shark eat for dinner?

Anything it wants.

What should you do if you see a blue whale?

Cheer it up.

How did the shark plead in court?

Not gill-ty.

79

Mountain
Mischief

How do wolves
greet each other?

"Howl do you do?"

Why wouldn't the moose
reveal its name?

It wanted to remain
anony-moose.

What's worse than
getting your hair
cut by a bear?

A close shave
with a gorilla.

81

What did the llama
see when it looked
in the mirror?

Its spitting image.

Did you hear about
the party of bears
in the mountains?

It was panda-monium.

I saw a cougar in
the wild once.

I nearly
puma pants.

Why did the alpacas panic?

Because the fire a-llamas went off.

Where do snow leopards like sleeping?

On Mount Ever-rest.

What did the goat say when it reached the top of the mountain?

"I have no idea how I goat here."

What does a panda use to make pancakes?

A pan, duh.

Llama 1: "I'm telling you, we're from South America."

Llama 2: "Peru-ve it."

What do alpacas call the end of the world?

The alpaca-lypse.

Why was the bald
eagle in a bad mood?

It kept losing
its hares.

What do you call
a celebrity elk?

Famoose.

Which two letters do you
need to spell 'panda'?

P and A.

Why do moose have such short tails?

Because there aren't any retail stores in the mountains.

Why was the little bear spoiled?

His mother panda'd to him.

Why did the mountain goat send her son back down the mountain?

Because he had a bad altitude.

What do wolves eat
for breakfast?

Woofles.

What do moose eat
for breakfast?

Moose-li.

What do mountain goats
eat for breakfast?

Weet-ibex.

Why was the sick eagle put in prison?

For ill-eagle activities.

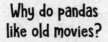

What happened when a group of mountain hares went missing?

The police had to comb the area.

Why do pandas like old movies?

Because they're in black and white.

Savanna Sniggers

Why shouldn't you play cards with cats in the savanna?

There are too many cheetahs.

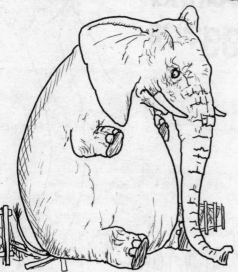

What time is it when an elephant sits on your fence?

Time to get a new fence.

Why can't a leopard hide?

Because it's always spotted.

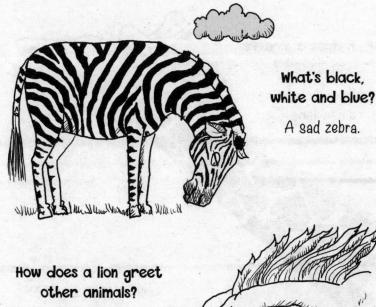

What's black, white and blue?

A sad zebra.

How does a lion greet other animals?

"Pleased to eat you."

What did the buffaloes say to their son when he went away?

"Bison!"

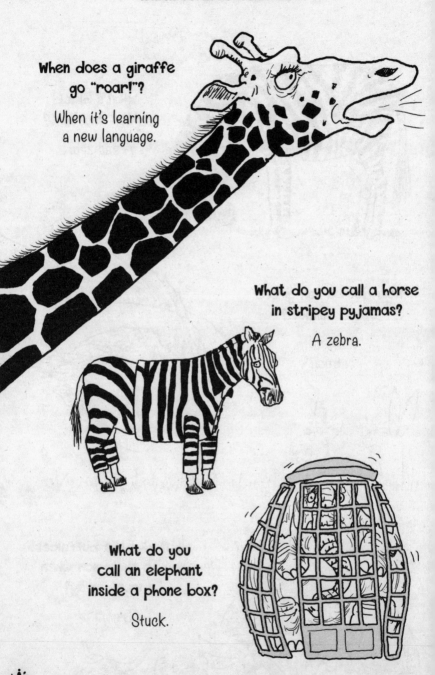

**When does a giraffe
go "roar!"?**

When it's learning
a new language.

**What do you call a horse
in stripey pyjamas?**

A zebra.

**What do you
call an elephant
inside a phone box?**

Stuck.

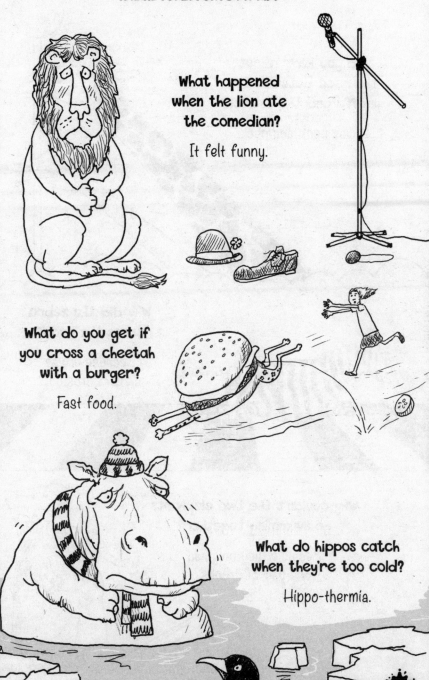

What happened when the lion ate the comedian?

It felt funny.

What do you get if you cross a cheetah with a burger?

Fast food.

What do hippos catch when they're too cold?

Hippo-thermia.

93

Did you hear about
the race between the
giraffe and the ostrich?

It was neck and neck.

Why did the zebra
cross the road?

Because it was
a zebra crossing.

Why couldn't the two elephants
go swimming together?

Because they only had
one pair of trunks.

94

What's an aardvark's favourite pizza topping?

Ant-chovies.

Why did the leopard go to the eye doctor?

Because it kept seeing spots.

What's a giraffe's favourite fruit?

Neck-tarines.

What's the difference between an Asian elephant and an African elephant?

About 5,000 miles.

What books do tortoises like to read?

Hardbacks.

How does a lion like its meat?

Roar!

96

What's worse than a giraffe with a sore throat?

An aardvark with a runny nose.

I was raised by a pack of hyenas.

The food was always scarce, but we had some great laughs.

Why are elephants wrinkled?

Because they take ages to iron.

97

Why did the hippo and the kangaroo form a band?

To make hip-hop music.

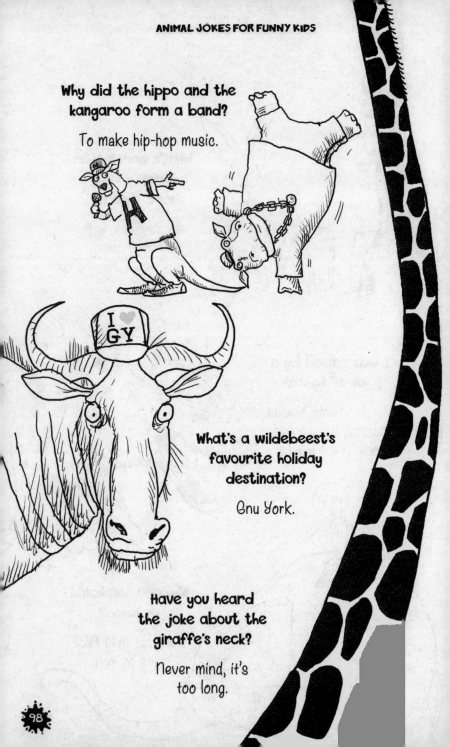

What's a wildebeest's favourite holiday destination?

Gnu York.

Have you heard the joke about the giraffe's neck?

Never mind, it's too long.

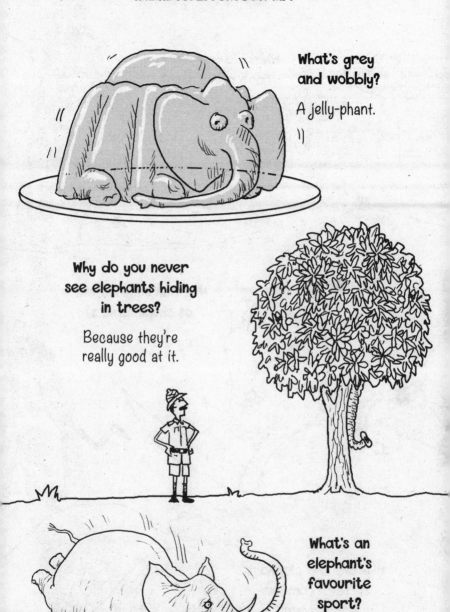

What's grey and wobbly?

A jelly-phant.

Why do you never see elephants hiding in trees?

Because they're really good at it.

What's an elephant's favourite sport?

Squash.

What do you call a lion's reflection?

A copycat.

Why can't rhinos work as shopkeepers?

They charge too much.

Why did the elephant suffer from low self-esteem?

It felt irrelephant.

Why don't giraffes make good pets?

They're too high maintenance.

Lion: "You're late, we said we'd meet at sunset."

Giraffe: "But I can still see the sun."

What happens when too many giraffes travel together?

There's a giraffic jam.

Polar
Pranks

Why don't polar bears and penguins get along?

Because they're polar opposites.

What do you call a horizontal walrus?

A floor-us.

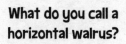

Why do seals have so many photo albums?

They're good at taking polaroids.

Why do narwhals always get invited to parties?

Because they're good at breaking the ice.

Where do penguins go to watch movies?

The dive-in.

How do Arctic hares keep their fur so white?

They use hare dye.

What's another name for an emperor penguin?

Julius Freezer.

Who's a seal's favourite pop star?

Seal-ena Gomez.

What's white, fuzzy and enjoys sunbathing?

A solar bear.

Why didn't the polar bear want to get married?

It got cold feet.

What's an Arctic hare's favourite drink?

A fur-appuccino.

Why are penguins good at using the internet?

Because they have web feet.

Have you heard the love story about the two young polar bears?

It was love at frost sight.

Why are penguins difficult to get along with?

Because they're always fishing for compliments.

What do seals use to make their beds?

Ice sheets and snow blankets

**What do you call a
happy penguin?**

A pen-grin.

**Where do walruses
go on holiday?**

Tusk-any.

**What do polar bears say
when they see tourists
in sleeping bags?**

"Mmm, burritos!"

**How do you close an
envelope in the Arctic?**

With a seal.

Why was the polar bear sad?

It was feeling ice-olated.

**How do penguins
make pancakes?**

With their flippers.

What do penguins wear on their summer holidays?

Ice caps and beak-inis.

How do you know if a bird is out of breath?

If it's puffin'.

What keeps the ocean from leaking?

Seals.

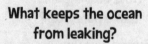

The polar bear had a lovely time on its summer holiday.

It was everything it thawed it would be.

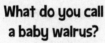

What do you call a baby walrus?

A small-rus.

How does a penguin build its house?

Igloos it together.

How do snowy owls communicate?

By winging each other.

What do penguins wear to keep their feet warm?

Slippers.

Why don't walruses tell seals their secrets?

Because seals are untuskworthy.

Why was the Arctic fox being watched by the police?

Because it was up to snow good.

What do penguins eat on their birthdays?

Fish cakes.

How do you treat an Arctic hare with a runny nose?

No bunny knows.

What's a polar bear's favourite food?

Brrrr-grrrrs.

Why can't penguins fly?

Because they're not tall enough to be pilots.

What's a seal's favourite subject?

Art! Art! Art!

114

Why do owls always get invited to parties?

Because they're a hoot.

What's a koala's favourite drink?

Coca-Koala.

How does a mouse feel after a bath?

Squeaky clean.

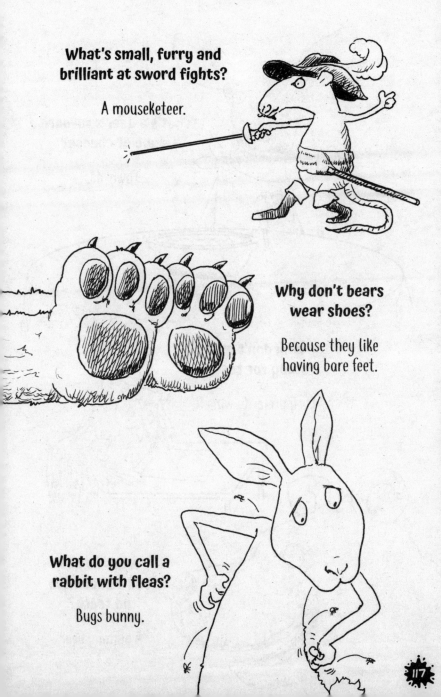

What's small, furry and brilliant at sword fights?

A mouseketeer.

Why don't bears wear shoes?

Because they like having bare feet.

What do you call a rabbit with fleas?

Bugs bunny.

What's a deer's favourite type of cheese?

Fawn-do.

Why don't owls study for tests?

They prefer to wing it.

What do you call a bear with no teeth?

A gummy bear.

What goes "dot, dot, dash, squeak"?

Mouse code.

Which tree did the squirrel visit on its holiday?

The beech.

Why are koalas good at getting hired?

They have lots of koalafications.

119

What do grizzly bears do to get through a bad day?

They grin and bear it.

How do you get a mouse to smile?

Say "cheese."

What do you call a bald porcupine?

Pointless.

What noise does a well-spoken owl make

"Whom."

Why did the squirrel get lost in the woods?

It followed the wrong root.

What do grizzly bears catch when they're sick?

Salmon-ella.

What did the mouse say to the ant as it crossed the street?

"Hello, fellow road-ant."

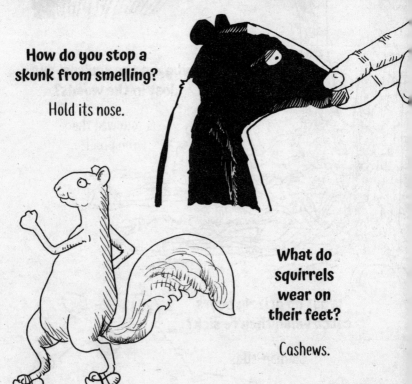

How do you stop a skunk from smelling?

Hold its nose.

What do squirrels wear on their feet?

Cashews.

What do you get if you cross a bear with a skunk?

Winnie the Pooh.

Why did the skunk start crying?

It was feeling scent-imental.

What did the judge say when the skunk walked into the courtroom?

"Odour in the court!"

What do you call
bears with no ears?

B.

Where do rabbits go
when they feel ill?

To the hops-ital.

What did the owl
say to the judge?

"I'm talon you,
it wasn't me."

What sort of joke would you hear a squirrel tell?

A-corny one.

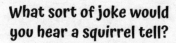

What happened to the grizzly bear when it rained?

It became a drizzly bear.

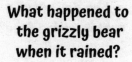

What do you call an owl in a bad mood?

A scowl.

What is it called when squirrels argue?

A squarrel.

What do you get when you cross a rabbit with a frog?

A bunny ribbit.

What dance did the fox do at the talent show?

The foxtrot.

Why do birds fly south in the winter?

Because it's too far to walk.

Why didn't the squirrel eat the macadamia nut?

Because it was a tough nut to crack.

How many skunks does it take to make a stink?

A phew.

127

ALSO
AVAILABLE:

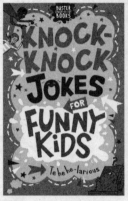

ISBN: 978-1-78055-785-4   ISBN: 978-1-78055-708-3

ISBN: 978-1-78055-626-0   ISBN: 978-1-78055-624-6   ISBN: 978-1-78055-625-3

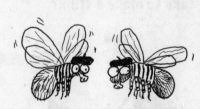